TANGOS, MILONGAS
and Other Latin-American Dances
for Solo Piano

Selected and with an Introduction
and Notes by
JOSEPH SMITH

DOVER PUBLICATIONS, INC.
Mineola, New York

ACKNOWLEDGMENTS

This collection was made possible only through the kind help of the following individuals and institutions. I am grateful to: Max Barros, Mirian Conti, Manoel Aranha Corrêa do Lago, Ana Maria Trenchi de Bottazzi, Graciela Penchaszadeh, David Witten; Richard Griscom and Leslie Troutman of the Music Library at the University of Illinois at Urbana-Champaign; Margo Gutiérrez at the Benson Latin American Collection of the University of Texas at Austin; Suzana Martins at the Rio de Janeiro Biblioteca Nacional; Jorge Matos Valldejuli at the Center for Puerto Rican Studies, Hunter College, New York; Maria Elena Tobón at the Americas Society, New York; the Music Division of the New York Public Library for the Performing Arts; Gabe M. Wiener Music and Arts Library of Columbia University; Stuart Isacoff; and especially to Mario Broeders, Valentine Surif, and Marcelo Verzoni. Finally, I would like to thank my editor, Ron Herder, for his unfailing kindness and support.

Copyright

Bibliographical Note

This Dover edition, first published in 2003, is a new compilation of works originally published separately. The introduction and notes were expressly written for this edition. The editors are grateful to Funarte Publishers for permission to reprint the Gomes selection, and to the quarterly *Piano Today* for permission to reprint the Ponce selection.

International Standard Book Number: 0-486-42787-0

Manufactured in the United States of America
Dover Publications, Inc., 31 East 2nd Street, Mineola, N.Y. 11501

INTRODUCTION

Dating from the late-nineteenth and early-twentieth centuries, all the pieces in this collection were written by Latin-American composers, based on rhythms of popular Latin-American dance music. All lie in that fascinating area in between "dance" and "concert" music—in other words, concert music in the form of dances, or dance music so inventive and culturally important that it asks to be brought into the concert hall! The collection contains examples from five different countries, and I hope that the reader will enjoy the chance to observe what musical elements they share, and yet how strongly each composer expresses a distinctive personality and national character. Of course, this collection can only provide a tiny glimpse of a vast literature of charming music that remains little known in North America.

JOSEPH SMITH

ABOUT THE EDITOR

The *New York Times* called pianist Joseph Smith's playing "eloquent," and the *Frankfurter Allgemeine Zeitung* found him a "richly sensitive interpreter." Mr. Smith has brought many little-known piano pieces to the attention of the public through performances, broadcasts, recordings, articles, anthologies, and lectures.

Smith is author of *Piano Discoveries* (Ekay Music), and editor of *Four Early 20th Century Piano Suites by Black Composers* (G. Schirmer), *American Piano Classics,* and *Country Gardens and other works for piano* (Dover). His articles on piano music have appeared in major periodicals, and his feature "Joseph Smith's Piano Bench" was heard monthly on National Public Radio's *Performance Today* for two years. His most recent CD is *Familiar Melodies— Transcriptions, Variations, and Fantasies* (Brioso).

Contents

IGNACIO MARÍA CERVANTES [KAWANAGH] (1847–1905) / **pp. 2–17**

brought new sophistication and refinement to the Cuban *danza*. At age seven, he played for famed North American virtuoso Louis Moreau Gottschalk, then on tour in Cuba, who encouraged him to pursue a career in music. Cervantes studied at the Paris Conservatory, winning a first prize in piano in 1866. As a result he became a regular performer at Rossini's famous salon. He returned to live in Havana in 1870, although he temporarily exiled himself to the U.S.A. when his sympathies for Cuban revolutionaries made him *persona non grata* with the Spanish authorities. A serious interpreter of Beethoven and Chopin, the modest Cervantes considered his danzas to be merely diversions.

Cervantes used to deliver little monologues in time to some of the danzas. Here are two examples, preserved by tradition:

EL VELORIO

Poor Juan . . . dead! Such a good family man . . .
Come on! Remember how he used to go dancing and eating chicken
and rice with all those people?
Oh! Please don't speak ill of him. Not now. God forgive him.

LA CELOSA

Four o'clock in the morning and my husband hasn't come home.
My parents were right about him after all. He'll come in lying—blaming his friends.
How nice—you finally show up! "Forgive me . . . my friends . . ."
Lies . . . "Listen" . . . I won't.
"Okay. Leave me alone, and let me get some sleep.
The heat . . . the mosquitoes . . . see you tomorrow."

Other of the danzas included here are enlivened with playful extramusical allusions.

Los tres golpes—The "three blows" are represented by the series of three accented chords which begins in the final eight bars.

¡Pst!—The *subito piano* in bar seven is the secretive call to attention.

¿Porche, eh?—The rhythm of the word "porque" is reflected in the two-note motif that appears throughout.

¡Te quiero tanto!—The final bars mark the rhythm of the phrase "te quiero tanto, te quiero tanto, te quiero tanto hasta morir" (I love you so, I'll love you until I die).

La carcajada—was inspired by the following incident: Cervantes was riding in a streetcar with an elderly lady wearing a bizarre hat. When the streetcar passed a group of girls, the girls burst into rude laughter upon seeing the hat. On the second page of this danza, the piano suddenly erupts in mocking *fortissimo* chords, interrupting the tune (and adding an extra bar to the phrase).

The Brazilian (ANTÔNIO) CARLOS GOMES (1836–1896) / pp. 18–21

is remembered as an opera composer. On the basis of his earliest operas, the government awarded him a scholarship to study at the Milan conservatory. His *Il Guarany,* produced at La Scala in 1870, achieved immediate international success—earning him the praise of both Boito and Verdi. While Italianate in its forms and robust flow of melody, his opera's shimmering texture of piquant orchestral and harmonic details evoke its ancient, exotic Brazilian setting. *Il Guarany* deals with Indian influence on Brazilian music; the hard-driving piano dance "A cayumba" celebrates the African influence.

JUAN MOREL CAMPOS (1857–1896) / pp. 22–49

spent his life teaching, conducting, and composing in Ponce, Puerto Rico, as well as making guest appearances in Brazil and Argentina. He was the protégé of Manuel Gregorio Tavárez, composer of one of the first published danzas. Tavárez had moved to Ponce to run the music department of a large store, then succeeded in turning it into an informal conservatory. His pupil Morel began composing danzas at age fourteen and never stopped. In his remaining 25 years, Morel Campos produced 339 examples, ranging from the capricious to the smolderingly passionate. (He also composed religious music, a zarzuela, and a symphony.) The range of Morel's danzas can be inferred from their piquant titles: the animals proceed from "The Microbe" to "The Alligator"; romance is celebrated in "To Live Is to Love" and deplored in "Damned Love!"; and the admonitions include "I Told You So" and "No, Don't Eat Matches." In the twentieth century, Morel's danzas enjoyed the advocacy of the great Puerto Rican pianist Jesús Maria Sanromá.

ERNESTO NAZARETH (1863–1934) / pp. 50–73

entitled one of his many Brazilian tangos "Cocky," and no single word could better convey the tone of his music in general. Nazareth had little formal training—he wished to study in Europe but was unable to raise the money. Nazareth became famous in Rio performing not in a formal concert hall but as a special attraction before the movie at the elegant Odeon Cinema. (He later toured Brazil.) He is said to have played his tangos not in strict dance tempo, but with rubatos and hesitations. Heitor Villa-Lobos admired him, calling Nazareth "the true incarnation of the Brazilian soul," and the two dedicated compositions to one another. Thus, Nazareth had a great, if indirect, influence on twentieth-century concert music. (One title requires explanation: "Nove de Julho," the ninth of July, is a holiday in Argentina. Here, the Brazilian composer pays tribute to the musical style of his neighbor country.)

MANUEL MARÍA PONCE (1882–1948) / pp. 74–75

Except for Gomes, the above composers are remembered primarily for their dances. The later composers in this collection, Ponce and Williams, however, belong more to the world of conventional "concert" music. The Mexican Manuel María Ponce is famous for guitar works popularized by Segovia, and for the sensationally successful song "Estrellita"—a tune so natural and inevitable-sounding that it would be easy to mistake for a folk song. Ponce's own and favorite instrument, however, was the piano, for which he composed extensively and idiomatically.

Most left-hand solos are composed either as technical studies or as concert pieces for injured pianists. Ponce's "Malgré tout," on the other hand, is a tribute to a sculptor. Jesús Contreras, born in Ponce's hometown of Aguascalientes, was a friend of the composer's. Contreras lost his right arm in an accident; shortly after, he sculpted a piece he named "Malgré tout" (Despite all). Ponce's tribute to this friend is also entitled "Malgré tout." Thus, the piece is a metaphor—and title, visual effect, and sound all contribute to its melancholy beauty.

José Ignacio Quintón (1881–1925) / pp. 76–98

reputed to be an excellent pianist, brought a new textural richness to the Puerto Rican danza. Although he composed concert works, both religious and instrumental, Quintón, unlike Morel Campos, synthesized popular idiom and virtuoso keyboard writing, as in his "Danzas de conciertos." Even his regular danzas, such as the ones included here, reflect a sophisticated pianism. It is not just that the pieces are more sonorous than earlier danzas—they are also more contrapuntal: the left hand, no longer confined to accompaniment patterns, is likely to share in the melodic interest. Three Quintón titles demand explanations: The word *coquí* (not to be found in Spanish dictionaries) refers to a small tree frog, which has risen to the status of beloved if unofficial symbol of Puerto Rico. Both its name and the ubiquitous two-octave leaps of Quintón's danza imitate its two-note rising call. The date of the ebullient "¡Viva la Union!" suggests that this danza is rejoicing in the formation of the "union" political party. At the end of a long rehearsal, one of Quintón's musicians exclaimed, "Se acabó el tereque" (a Puerto Rican idiom meaning "done with it"), and this was adopted as the title of the new danza they had been playing.

Manuel Saumell [Robredo] (1817–1870) / page 99

an unpretentious, versatile, and pragmatic musician—lived by scrambling from one ill-paying job to another, arranging, composing, and playing a variety of instruments. An ardent musical nationalist, he once began a Cuban opera, but is best remembered today as the father of the Cuban *contradanza*. (This term, often shortened to *danza,* is believed to derive from the English *country dance.*) His surviving compositions are all in the form of short contradanzas and exemplify a variety of Cuban rhythms.

Few musicians have so profoundly benefited their country in as many respects as the Argentinian **Alberto Williams (1862–1952) / pp. 100–116.** (The paternal branch of his family was British.) Trained at the Paris Conservatory and a student of César Franck, Williams returned to Argentina in 1889. He performed as pianist and conductor, initiated several concert series, and founded the Buenos Aires Conservatory (now the Conservatorio Williams), bringing a new seriousness and professionalism to Argentina's musical life. His concert tours took him to different provinces, exposing him to local styles of folk music. From the 1890s on, he made use of these idioms in compositions which eventually reached the opus number of 136 and include nine symphonies! In his wealth of piano dances, Williams manages to reflect contemporary European influences in their harmonic and pianistic subtlety (for instance, the silent re-taking of notes in the *Hueya* republished here) without compromising their local dance character. The milonga is a ballroom dance, whereas the hueya (the word means the "usual" steps) is a gaucho (cowboy) dance. The titles of the Milongas are in gaucho vernacular, and have erotic connotations, as suggested in the English explanations on the contents page.

"Elastic Triplets"

Some of the Puerto Rican danzas present a question of rhythmic performance practice—the so-called *tresillos elasticos* ("elastic triplets"). A triplet may represent a simplified notation for a syncopated rhythm. For example—to quote from three pieces by Morel Campos—the accompaniment "triplets" in "Felices dias" (p. 37, third system) are likely intended to be played as . . .

. . . and the quarter-note triplets in the prelude of "Alma sublime" (p. 22) as. . .

Certainly, however, when left-hand triplets accompany triplets in a right-hand melody, it is clear that "real" triplets are intended, as in "¡No me toques!" (p. 46):

The execution of triplets in the Puerto Rican danza remains a subject of dispute among scholars, and the player may be guided by his or her preference.

GLOSSARY OF MUSICAL TERMS

Simple respellings of such familiar Italian terms as *staccato*
have been omitted from this basic list.

alegrement, happily

ao trio, go to the trio

baixo, bass

bem jocoso, very playful

bem ligado = molto legato

com alma, with feeling

com graça, gracefully

chula, a Brazilian dance characterized by violent
    choreography, clapping hands and tapping feet

fim = Fine (end)

gingando, swinging

menos, less

0 baixo bem marcado e ligado, the bass very marked
    and smooth

para acabar, to the end

sapateado, tapping the feet

sentito, with feeling

só para acabar, only in order to end

zinguezagueando, zigzagging

TANGOS, MILONGAS

and Other Latin-American Dances
for Solo Piano

La carcajada
(The peal of laughter)

Ignacio Cervantes

La celosa

(The jealous woman)

Ignacio Cervantes

marcato il basso

Gran señora
(Grande dame)

Ignacio Cervantes

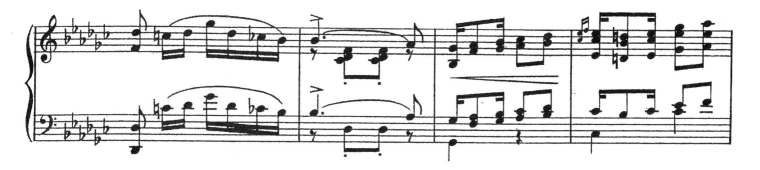

Invitación
(Invitation)

Ignacio Cervantes

Moderato con espressione.

¡No lloras más!
(Weep no more!)

Ignacio Cervantes

Con tenerezza.

¿Porche, eh?

(Why, eh?)

Ignacio Cervantes

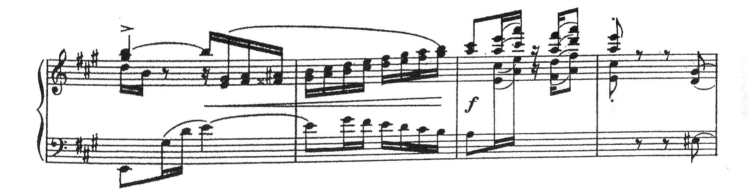

¡Pst!

Ignacio Cervantes

Poco vivo con spirito.

Se fué y no vuelve más

(Is gone and shall not return)

Ignacio Cervantes

¡Te quiero tanto!

(I love you so much!)

Ignacio Cervantes

Moderato melanconico.

Los tres golpes
(The three blows)

Ignacio Cervantes

El velorio

(The wake)

Ignacio Cervantes

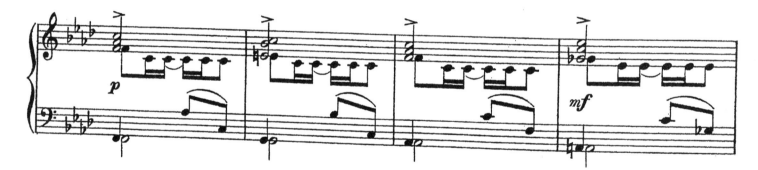

A cayumba: Dança dos negros

(The cayumba: African-Brazilian dance of Blacks)

Antônio Carlos Gomes

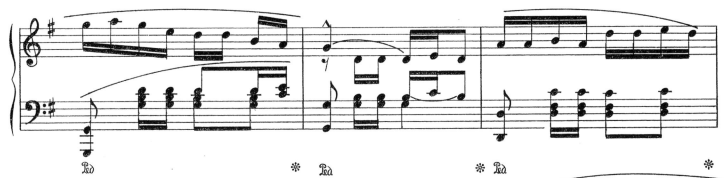

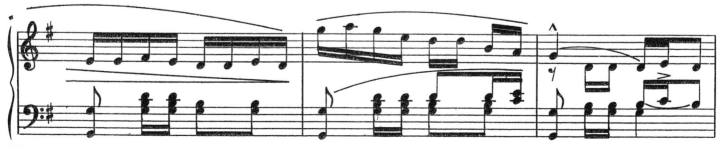

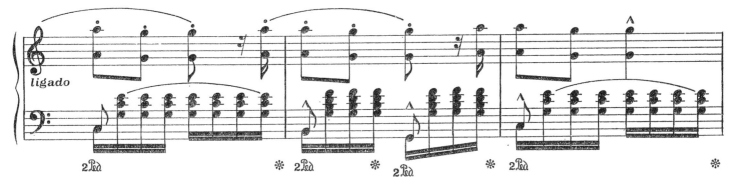

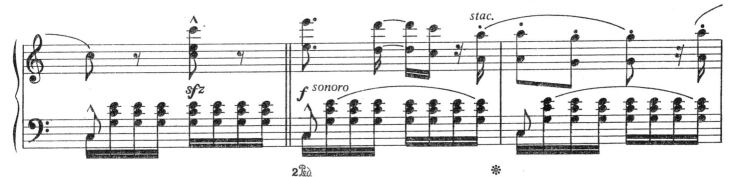

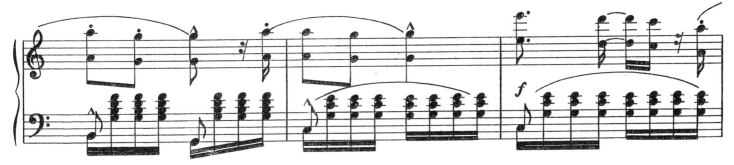

Alma sublime
(Sublime soul)

Juan Morel Campos

¡Ausencia!
(Absence!)

Juan Morel Campos

¡Buen humor!
(Good humor!)

Cielo de encantos

(Heaven of charms)

Juan Morel Campos

¡Dí que me amas!

(Say that you love me!)

Juan Morel Campos

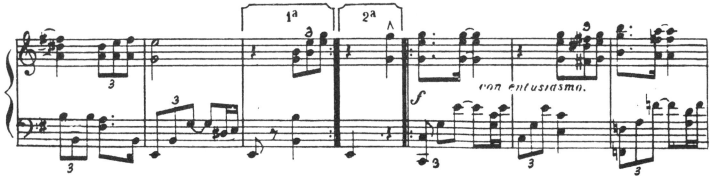

Felices dias
(Happy days!)

Juan Morel Campos

¡Feliz encuentro!

(Fortunate encounter!)

Juan Morel Campos

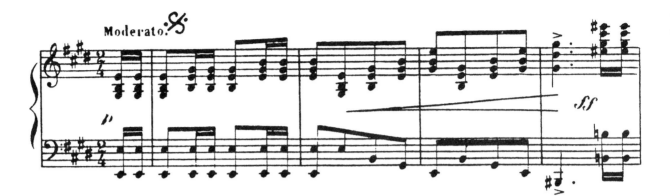

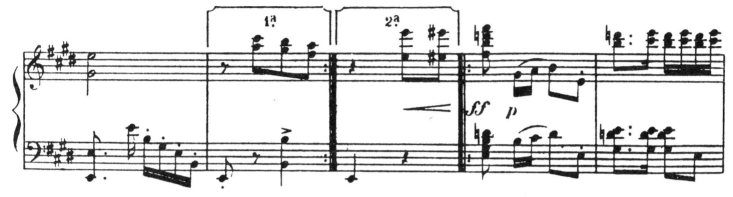

Idilio
(Idyl)

Juan Morel Campos

44 *Morel Campos*

¡No me toques!
(Don't touch me!)

Juan Morel Campos

¡Si te toco!

(Yes, I touch you!)

Juan Morel Campos

Digo
(I say)

Ernesto Nazareth

Alegremente.

D.C.%.

Famoso
(Famous)

Ernesto Nazareth

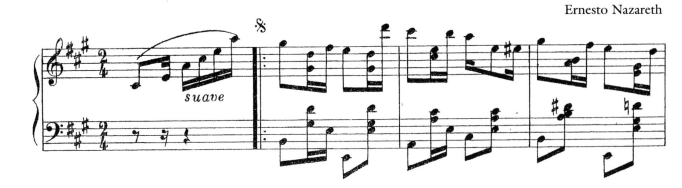

Guerreiro
(Fighter)

Ernesto Nazareth

TRIO

p *Sapateado*

cresc.........

ben stacato il basso

f

p

cresc.....

f

ff

molto legato

I.

2.

rit.

p

mf

D.C. al 𝄋

Myosotis
(Forget-me-not)

Ernesto Nazareth

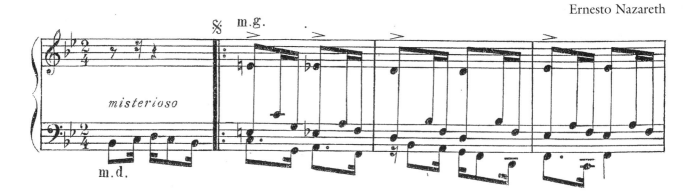

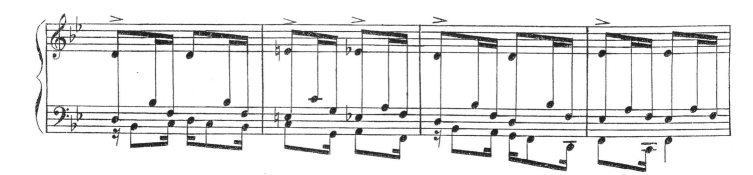

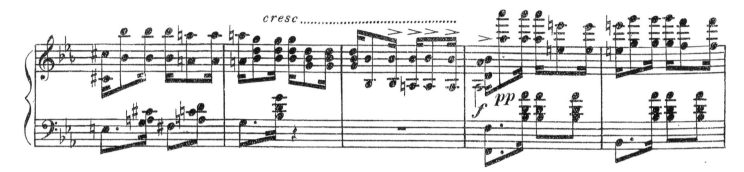

D.C.ao 𝄋

Nove de Julho

(The ninth of July)

Ernesto Nazareth

p delicadissimo

com graça   rit.

a tempo

simples

TRIO

Bem jocoso

Baixo f

D.C. al 𝄋

Pierrot

Ernesto Nazareth

D.C. 𝄋.

Nazareth 69

Talisman
(Lucky charm)

Ernesto Nazareth

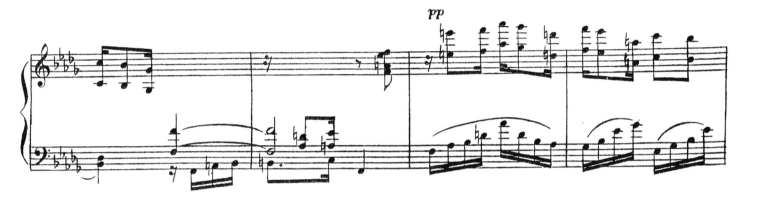

cres. . . . . . . _f_

dim.

sempre   *p   mysterioso*

D.C. al

Malgré tout
(Despite all)

Manuel María Ponce

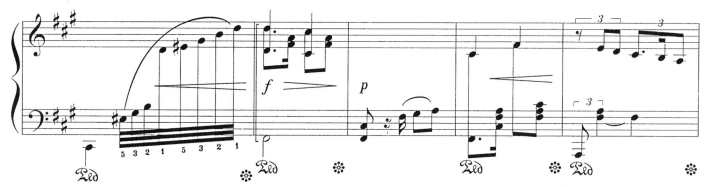

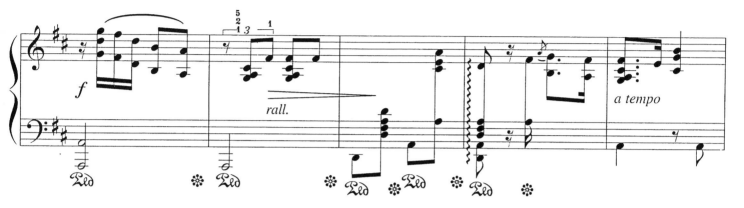

El coquí

(The tree frog)

José Ignacio Quintón

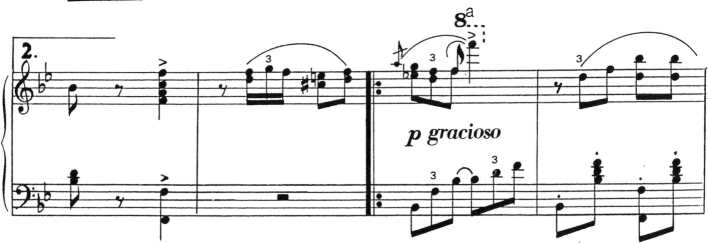

espresivo

p grazioso

p

Mascota
(Mascot)

José Ignacio Quintón

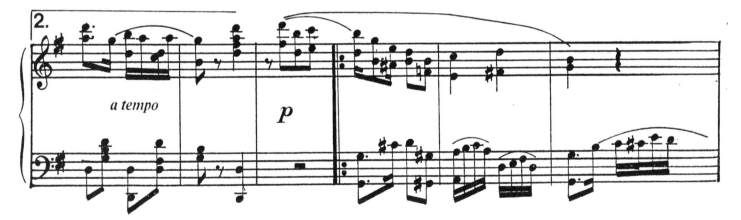

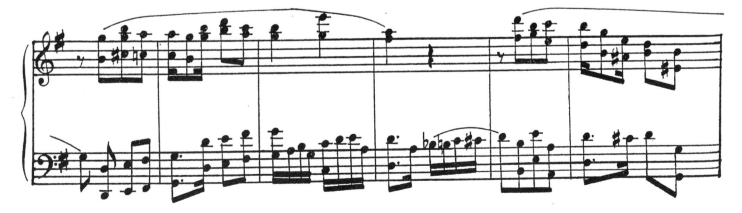

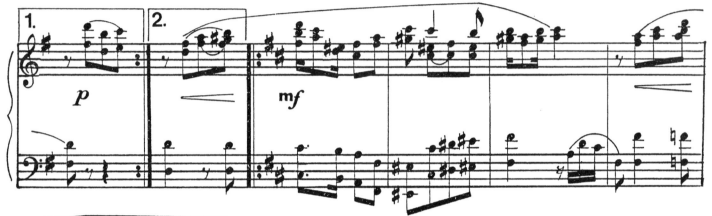

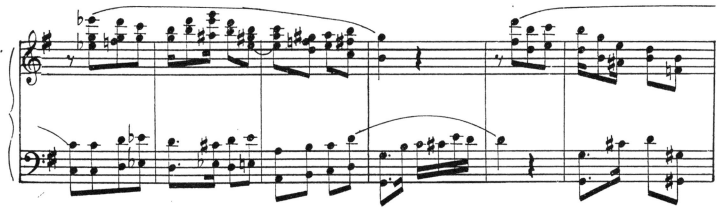

cresc — — — — cen — — — — do

ff

Se acabó el tereque
(Done with it!)

José Ignacio Quint

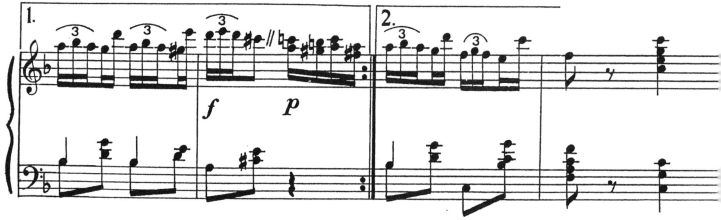

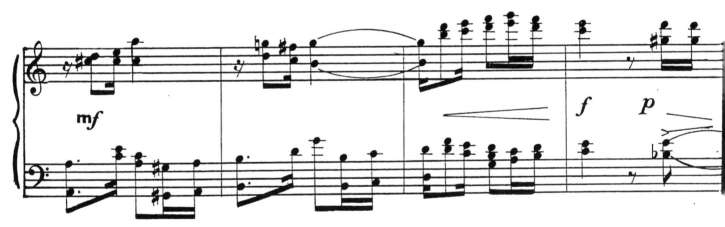

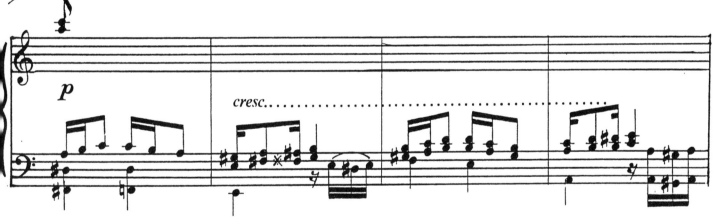

Si fueras mía

(If you were mine)

José Ignacio Quintón

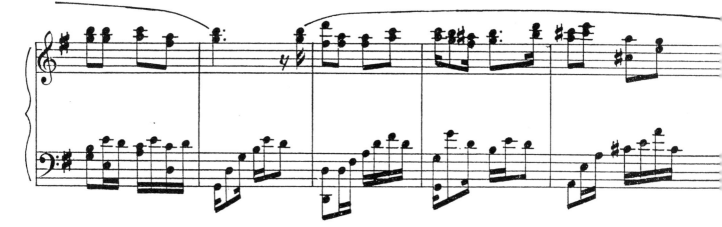

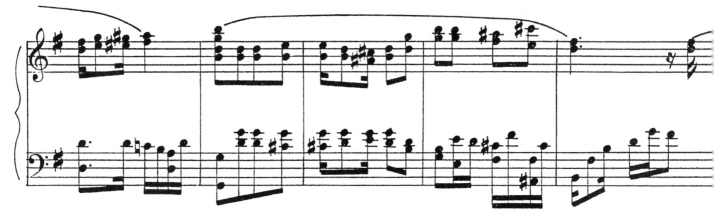

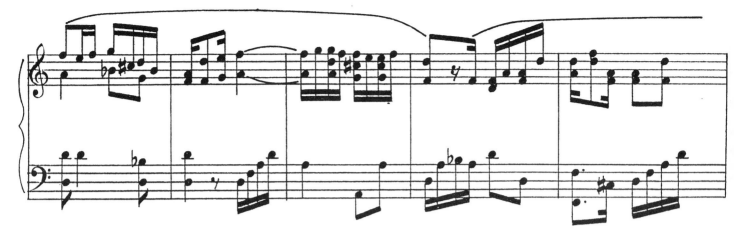

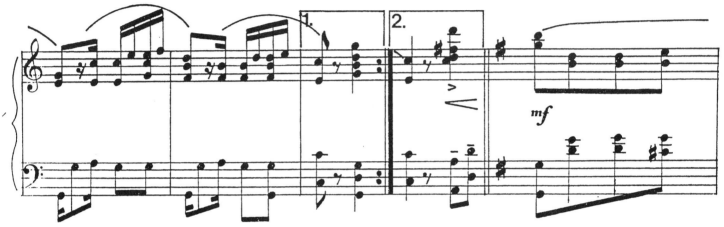

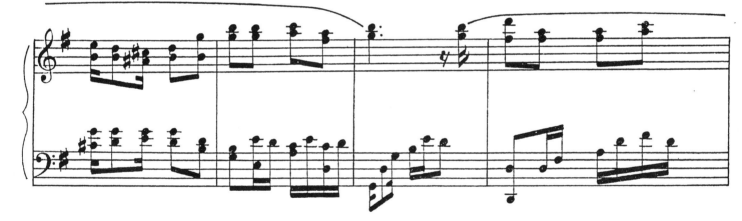

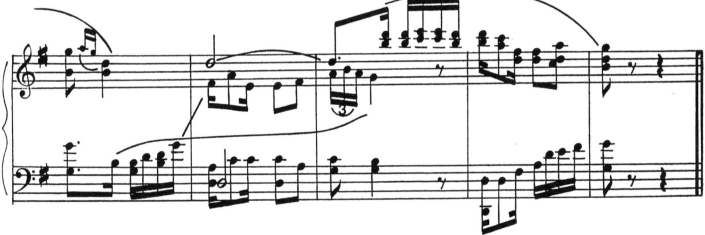

¡Viva la Unión!
(Long live the Union!)

José Ignacio Quintón

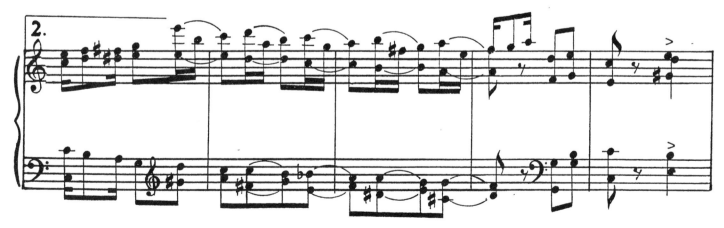

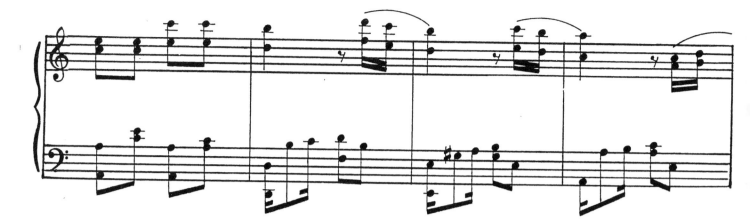

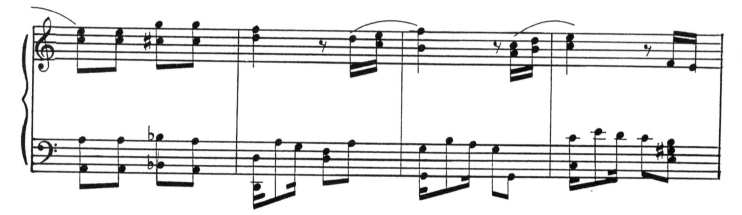

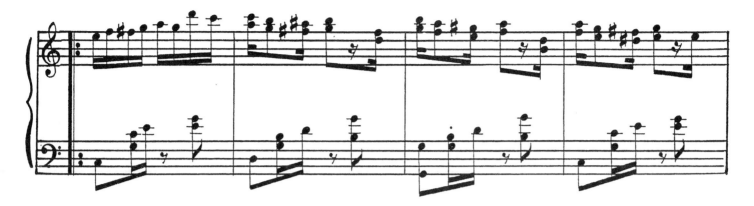

El ultimo golpe
(The final blow)

Manuel Saumell

Hueya
Op. 46, No. I

Alberto Williams

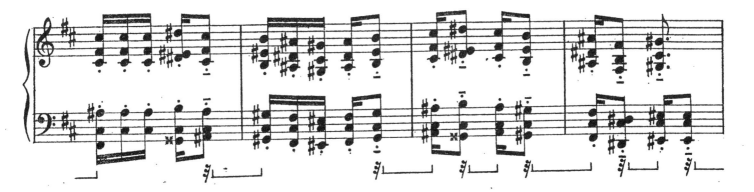

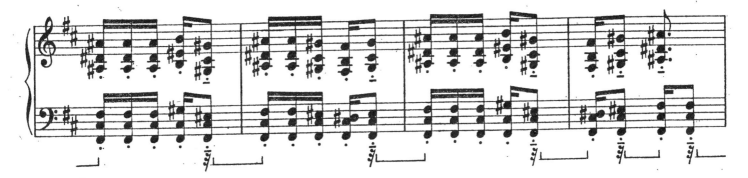

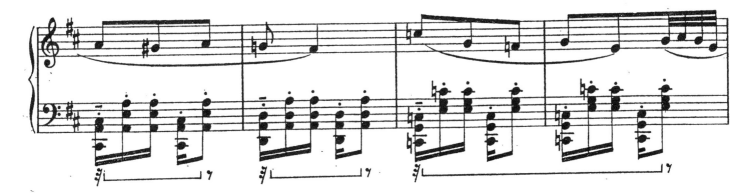

a tempo

p cantando

p cresc.

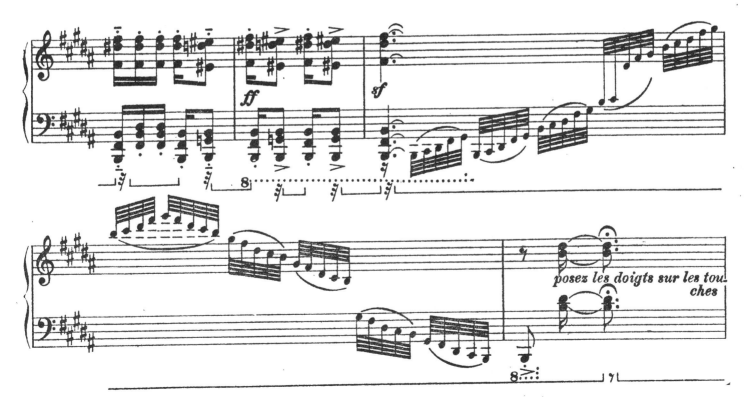

ff

sf

posez les doigts sur les tou-
ches

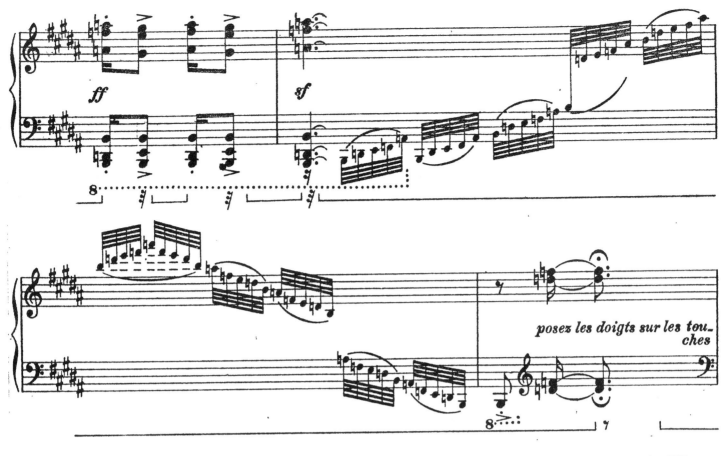

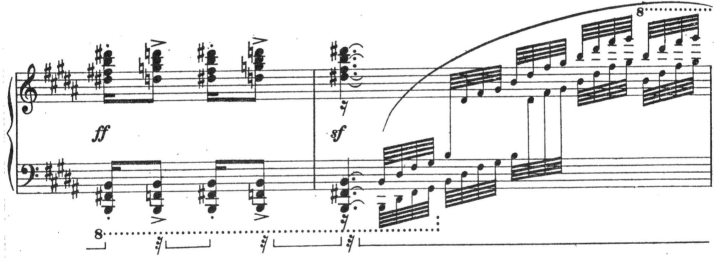

Requiebro a las caderas

(Admiring her hips)

No. 4 from *Milongas*, Op. 63

Alberto Williams

[The title refers to the sensual movements of a woman dancing the Argentinan *zamba*.]

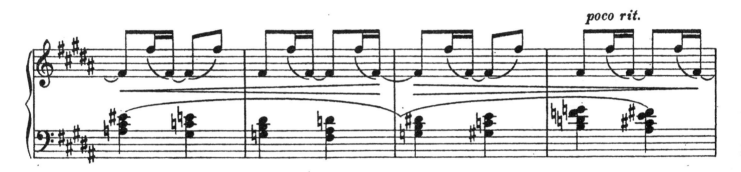

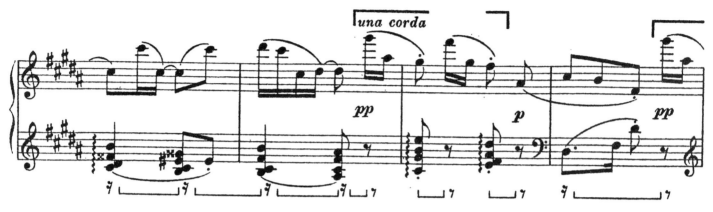

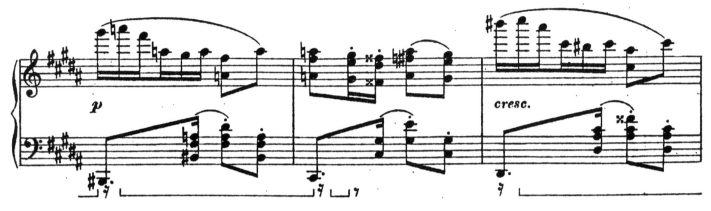

La rodaja de mi espuela
se ha enredado en tu pollera
(The wheel of my spur is tangled in your skirt)
No. 6 from *Milongas,* Op. 63

Alberto Williams

¡Qué trenzas para pialar payadores!

(What braids to lasso the payadores!)

No. 9 from *Milongas*, Op. 63

Alberto Williams

[The *payadores* are guitar-playing troubadours of the pampas
who compete with one another with story and song.]

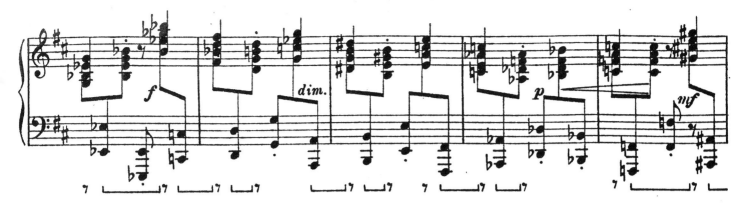

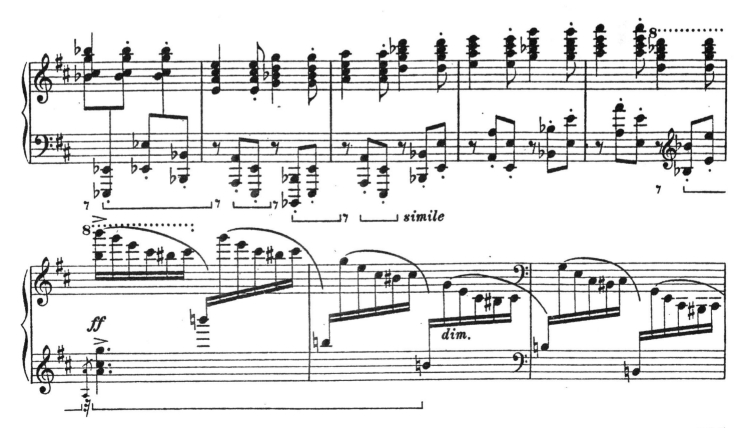